D1568679

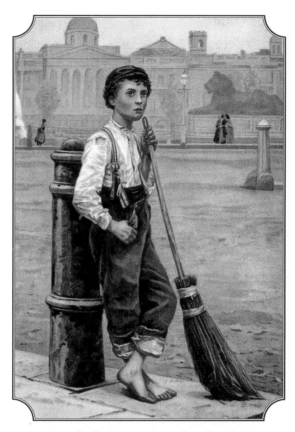

THE CITY

LIFE IN VICTORIAN ENGLAND

THE CITY

VIRGINIA SCHOMP

MARSHALL CAVENDISH • BENCHMARK
NEW YORK

In loving memory of Rosemary A. Leonardo

The author and publishers would like to thank Walter L. Arnstein, Professor of History Emeritus at the University of Illinois at Urbana-Champaign, for his valuable comments and careful reading of the manuscript.

This publication represents the opinions and views of the author based on Virginia Schomp's personal experience, knowledge, and research. The information in this book serves as a general guide only. The author and publisher have used their best efforts in preparing this book and disclaim liability rising directly and indirectly from the use and application of this book.

Other Marshall Cavendish Offices: Marshall Cavendish International (Asia) Private Limited, 1 New Industrial Road, Singapore 536196 • Marshall Cavendish International (Thailand) Co Ltd. 253 Asoke, 12th Flr, Sukhumvit 21 Road, Klongtoey Nua, Wattana, Bangkok 10110, Thailand • Marshall Cavendish (Malaysia) Sdn Bhd, Times Subang, Lot 46, Subang Hi-Tech Industrial Park, Batu Tiga, 40000 Shah Alam, Selangor Darul Ehsan, Malaysia

Marshall Cavendish is a trademark of Times Publishing Limited
All websites were available and accurate when this book was sent to press.

LIBRARY OF CONGRESS CATALOGING-IN-PUBLICATION DATA Schomp, Virginia. The city / by Virginia Schomp. p. cm. — (Life in Victorian England) Includes bibliographical references and index. Summary: "Describes daily life in the cities of England during the reign of Queen Victoria (1837-1901), from the poor, to the middle classes, to the upper classes, with a focus on the lives of women and children as well as men"—Provided by publisher. ISBN 978-1-60870-029-5 1. Great Britain—History—Victoria, 1837-1901—Juvenile literature. 2. Great Britain—Social conditions—19th century—Juvenile literature. 3. City and town life—England—History—19th century—Juvenile literature. I. Title. DA550.S35 2011 307.760941'09034—dc22 2009036710

EDITOR: Joyce Stanton PUBLISHER: Michelle Bisson ART DIRECTOR: Anahid Hamparian SERIES DESIGNER: Michael Nelson

Photo research by Rose Corbett Gordon, Art Editor of Mystic CT The photographs in this book are used by permission and through the courtesy of: Cover: Tate Gallery/Art Resource, NY Back cover: akg-images/Archie Miles Pages 1, 21, 34, 39, 64: Mary Evans Picture Library/The Image Works; pages 2-3: Museum of London/Bridgeman Art Library; page 7: Private Collection/Bourne Gallery, Reigate, Surrey/Bridgeman Art Library; pages 8, 15, 24, 50: The Art Archive/John Meek; page 11: The Print Collector/HIP/The Image Works; pages 13, 16: Stapleton Collection/HIP/The Image Works; pages 14, 32 top, 56: Private Collection/Bridgeman Art Library; page 18: Manchester Art Gallery/Bridgeman Art Library; page 20: Corporation of London/HIP/The Image Works; page 23: The Stapleton Collection/Bridgeman Art Library; page 26: England©NMPFT/SSPL/The Image Works; page 29: City of Westminster England ©Oxford Science Archive/HIP/The Image Works; page 32 bottom: The Art Archive; page 33: Victoria & Albert Museum/Art Resource, NY; page 36: The Art Archive/Eileen Tweedy; page 40: Topham/The Image Works; pages 42, 61, 69: HIP/Art Resource, NY; page 43: The Art Archive/Harper Collins Publishers; page 44: Hulton-Deutsch Collection/Corbis; pages 46, 54, 57: Fine Art Photographic Library/Corbis; page 48: Roy Miles Fine Paintings/Bridgeman Art Library; page 53: The Boston Athenaeum; page 58: akg images/Archie Miles; page 62: Stapleton Collection/Corbis; page 67: The Art Archive/Erin Pauwels Collection; page 71: Private Collection/Look and Learn/Bridgeman Art Library.

Printed in Malaysia (T)
135642

Front cover: *St. Martin-in-the-Fields* by William Logsdail portrays a young flower seller in London's Trafalgar Square.
Half-title page: A barefoot crossing sweeper
Title page: Passengers travel through Victorian London on a horse-drawn omnibus.
Back cover: A photograph of an upper-class boy dressed up in a fussy "Little Lord Fauntleroy" costume

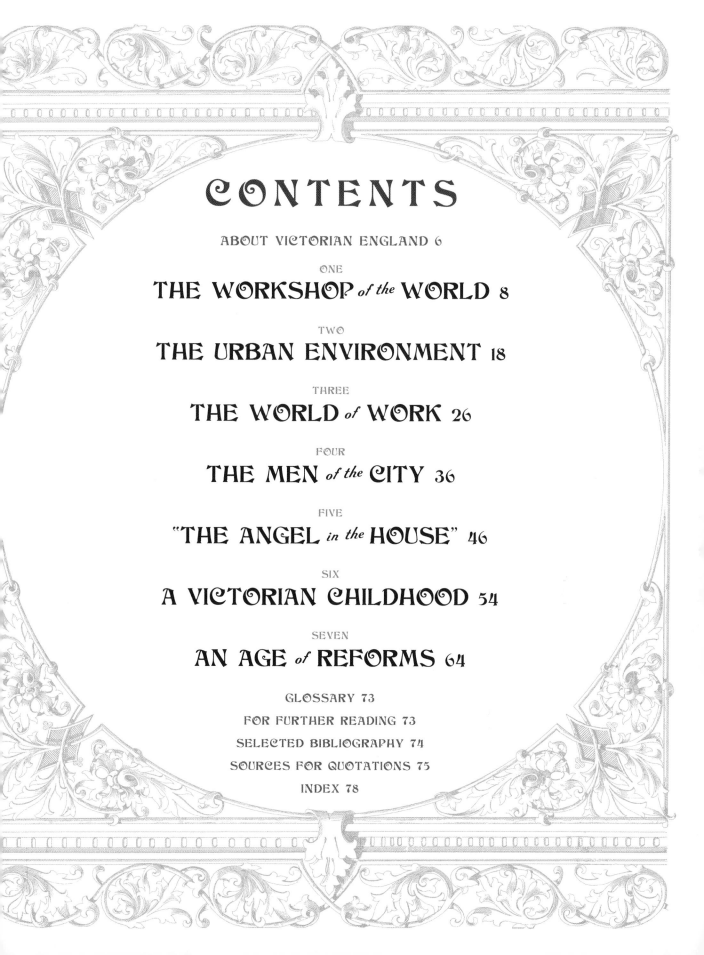

CONTENTS

ABOUT VICTORIAN ENGLAND

ON JUNE 20, 1837, KING WILLIAM IV OF ENGLAND DIED, and his eighteen-year-old niece, Victoria, ascended the throne. The teenage queen recorded her thoughts in her diary:

> Since it has pleased Providence to place me in this station, I shall do my utmost to fulfil my duty towards my country; I am very young and perhaps in many, though not in all things, inexperienced, but I am sure, that very few have more real good will and more real desire to do what is fit and right than I have.

That blend of faith, confidence, devotion to duty, and the earnest desire to do good would guide Victoria through the next sixty-three years and seven months, the longest reign of any English monarch. The queen's personal qualities would also set the tone for the period that bears her name, the Victorian Age.

Today the term *Victorian* is sometimes used to describe someone who is prim and prudish. We may think of Queen Victoria as a stuffy old lady presiding over a long, formal dinner party where everyone watches their language and worries about which fork to use. That image is not entirely wrong. Victoria and her subjects *did* believe in "traditional values" such as duty, discipline, and self-control. Their society *was* governed by a set of strict moral and social rules. However, that is not the whole picture. When we look deeper, we discover that the Victorian era, far from being dull and predictable, was a period of extraordinary growth and change. Between 1837 and 1901, England was transformed from a mostly agricultural, isolated society into a modern industrial nation with territories all over the world. The Victorian people witnessed astonishing advances in science and technology, as well as sweeping political, legal, and social reforms. A Victorian physician named Sir Henry Holland described his exciting times as "an age of transition, a period when changes, deeply and permanently affecting the whole condition of mankind, are occurring more rapidly, as well as extensively, than at any prior time in human history."

Life in Victorian England takes a look at this dynamic era, with a focus on the people and their everyday lives. The four books in the series will introduce us to men, women, and children at all levels of society, from poor farmers and factory workers to striving middle-class families to the aristocrats at the top of the social scale. In this volume we will meet the ladies and gentlemen, clerks and tradespeople, servants, laborers, peddlers, and paupers who jammed the streets of England's booming industrial cities. We will see where these people lived and worked, how they raised their children, and how they responded to the challenges of their times.

Buying a New Hat by Joseph Clark

Now it is time to step back to a world that is poised on the brink of the modern age. Welcome to an era when gas lamps are giving way to electric lightbulbs, stagecoaches to locomotives, wooden sailing vessels to iron warships. Welcome to life in Victorian England!

PENN & SONS
ENGINEERS
GREENWICH

Victorian factories built
the giant steam engines
that powered Britain's
first ironclad warships.

ONE

THE WORKSHOP
of the WORLD

Our country has become emphatically a land of great cities.
⟶ ROBERT VAUGHAN, *THE AGE OF GREAT CITIES* (1843)

FOR MOST OF HUMAN HISTORY, PEOPLE MADE THINGS by hand. Women spun thread, wove cloth, and sewed their family's clothing. Farmers raised crops with the help of simple handmade tools and animal-driven plows. Shoes, hats, pots, utensils, furniture—nearly everything was made by ordinary people in their homes or by skilled craftspeople in small workshops.

In the early 1700s, the way people lived and worked began to change. British inventors led the way, developing machines to speed up the production of textiles. The flying shuttle, invented by John Kay, allowed weavers to work faster. James Hargreaves's spinning jenny, Richard Arkwright's water frame, and Samuel Crompton's spinning mule brought further advances to spinning and weaving.

During the 1760s, the Scottish inventor James Watt worked on improving the new steam pumps that were being used to drain water from coal mines. Around 1784 he succeeded in developing an efficient steam engine that could drive many different kinds of machinery. Soon steam was powering locomotives, riverboats, and laborsaving textile machines. The cloth that people had made by hand could now be produced more quickly and cheaply by machines housed in large textile factories. It was a turning point in history, the start of the Industrial Revolution.

There were a number of reasons behind Great Britain's leading role in the Industrial Revolution. The nation had a strong economy. It had an abundance of coal, iron ore, water, and other natural resources and raw materials needed for production. Its network of territories and colonies, along with former colonies such as the United States, provided additional raw materials plus a market for finished goods. Britain also had a large and growing population. During the Victorian Age, its population would more than double, from about 18.5 million to 40 million. Many of these people would pour into the new manufacturing centers. Their migration would transform British society and city life forever.

THE URBAN EXPLOSION

In 1801 about 20 percent of the population of England and Wales lived in large towns or cities. Fifty years later, that figure had climbed to 54 percent. The upward trend would continue through the rest of the century until, by 1901, nearly 80 percent of the British people were city dwellers.

The growth of the cities was largely a consequence of the Industrial Revolution. Life was a constant struggle in the English countryside. Most farmers toiled for wealthy landowners in return for low,

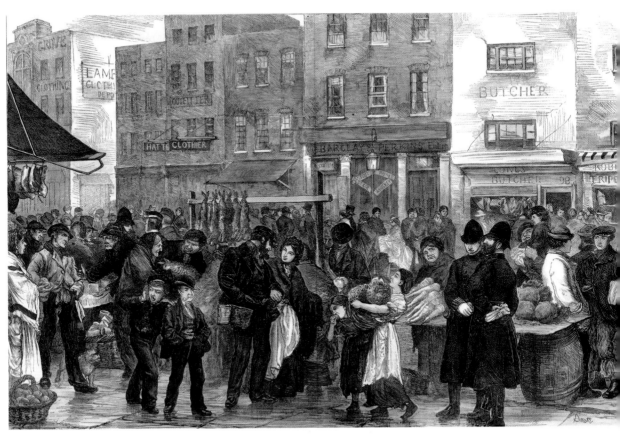

unreliable wages. The new manufacturing centers offered a chance to escape from this hand-to-mouth existence. As people moved from the countryside to work in factories, mills, and mines, the population of many small towns exploded.

Some towns expanded faster than others. Between 1801 and 1851, Liverpool grew from a small seaside town of about 80,000 people to a large port city with a population over 375,000. The same period saw the population triple in Birmingham, a leader in metalworking, and quadruple in Manchester, center of the textile industry. Other rapidly expanding cities included Bradford, Bristol, Sheffield, and Leeds in England and Glasgow in Scotland.

England's capital was in a league all its own. At the start of the Victorian Age, London was already the largest city in the world. Over

Buyers, sellers, and idlers fill a crowded, noisy marketplace in Victorian London.

the next sixty years, its population would skyrocket from nearly 2 million to an unheard-of 6.5 million. This rapid growth was not due to industrialization alone. In fact, during the Industrial Revolution, London fell behind several other cities in activities such as textile production and shipbuilding. Nevertheless, it remained the all-important center of British government, law, trade, and banking. An endless stream of products flowed in and out of its busy international ports. London was also the hub of the new railway network transforming the face of England.

RAILWAY MANIA

In 1825 the first public railway, the Stockton to Darlington line, chugged its way across northeast England. Five years later, the Liverpool and Manchester Railway opened, making a tidy profit carrying cargo and passengers between those two fast-growing cities. Suddenly, people realized that there was a fortune to be made in the new form of transportation. "Railway mania" swept the country, with private companies scrambling to open their own passenger lines. By 1850, more than six thousand miles of iron railway tracks crisscrossed England.

Before the coming of the railways, long-distance travel had been restricted to those who could afford to own private carriages or purchase fares on public stagecoaches. Train travel was for everyone. Every railroad was required by law to run at least one low-fare train a day, charging passengers no more than a penny a mile, with reduced rates for children. Suddenly, villagers who had never ventured more than a few miles from home could travel nearly anywhere in the country.

Railway mania also helped fuel the growth of business and industry. Freight trains whisked perishable goods such as milk from coun-

Cargo was transported from the Liverpool docks through Wapping Tunnel, the first railway tunnel built beneath the streets of a city.

try farms to towns and cities. They offered a fast, inexpensive way to transport raw materials to factories and finished products to markets and seaports. Ancient towns without rail access dwindled, while towns and villages along the transport routes prospered.

Not everyone welcomed the transportation revolution. Some critics complained about the noisy, smoky locomotives and the invasion of tracks, tunnels, and embankments into unspoiled landscape. Most Victorians, however, viewed the railways as a proud symbol of progress and achievement.

To both supporters and critics, it was clear that the railways marked the beginning of a new era. "*Then* was the old world," wrote the English novelist William Makepeace Thackeray in 1860. "Stage-coaches, more or less swift, riding-horses, pack-horses, highway-men, knights in armour, . . . and so forth—all these belong to the old period. . . . But your railroad starts the new era. . . . We are of the age of steam."

A PATCHWORK OF GOVERNMENTS

The growth of cities meant more jobs, more opportunities, more variety and excitement in the lives of the British people. At the same time, it brought a host of problems. Towns were unprepared

Many poor city dwellers drew their water from polluted streams and rivers.

for the rapid increases in population and industry. They grew haphazardly, with housing springing up like weeds among factories, warehouses, and railway yards. Public services were quickly overwhelmed. Wells and fountains that had supplied freshwater to 50,000 people could not keep up with the demands of two or three times that many. Cesspits—holes that held human waste—overflowed into the surrounding ground and water supplies.

At first, Britain's government did little to address such problems. Under the system of government that the early Victorians inherited, it was hard for political leaders to enact the sweeping reforms that were needed. Parliament was in charge of governing the nation. It passed laws, administered justice, and oversaw national defense and foreign relations. The real power in the day-to-day lives of most people, however, rested with the officials of local governments.

The basic unit of local government was the parish. In the 1830s Great Britain was divided into some 15,000 parishes, ranging in size from a few clusters of country cottages to large city neighborhoods. Local authorities presided over the affairs of each parish. They were responsible for keeping the peace, judging legal cases, maintaining the roads, providing relief to the poor, and dealing with other local matters.

This patchwork of local governments was unprepared to deal with the complex challenges of rapid industrialization. Some officials struggled to find solutions to problems such as overcrowding, homelessness, and poor sanitation. More often, all the different governing bodies in a large town or city bickered over their own rights and responsibilities while conditions deteriorated.

The absence of effective government policies left industrialists free to operate however they wanted. A city's leading business owners could build and manage mills, factories, warehouses, and workers' housing in the most profitable manner, without concern for living or working conditions. Their wealth and influence gave them the power to crush all attempts to interfere with their private interests on behalf of the public good.

It would take the people of Victorian England several decades to come to grips with these difficult issues. Reformers would gradually realize that the new problems of industrialization could only be solved with new weapons. They would have to change the way government operated at both the local and national levels. Parliament in particular would have to be "radically altered, and endowed with new powers," urged the British physician and reformer John Snow. Above all, it would need the power of "doing away with that form of liberty to which some communities cling, the sacred power to poison to death not only themselves but their neighbors."

A family scrapes out a meager living selling odds and ends in the slums of London.

CHARLES DICKENS AND THE RAILWAY

Many of our images of Victorian England come from the writings of Charles Dickens. Born in Portsmouth, England, in 1812, Dickens experienced the Industrial Revolution firsthand. His novels, short stories, and essays paint a vivid portrait of the people and places of his times. *Oliver Twist*, *David Copperfield*, *Great Expectations*, *A Christmas Carol*—through these and other Dickens classics, we can visit Victorian cities, schools, and factories, in the company of wily pickpockets, plucky orphans, greedy industrialists, and other colorful characters.

Charles Dickens also gave us some of the first and liveliest descriptions of the railways. An enthusiastic supporter of science and technology, he was convinced that the advances in transportation would change people's lives for the better. In the following description of a journey from London to the countryside, Dickens captured the somewhat alarming thrill of high-speed travel.

Above: A steam-powered train chugs its way across the green, boggy countryside outside Manchester.

Ah! The fresh air is pleasant . . . though it does blow over these interminable streets, and scatter the smoke of this vast wilderness of chimneys. Here we are—no, I mean there we were, for it has darted far into the rear—in Bermondsey where the tanners live. Flash! The distant shipping in the Thames is gone. Whirr! The little streets of new brick and red tile, with here and there a flagstaff growing like a tall weed out of the scarlet beans. . . . Whizz! Dust-heaps, market-gardens, and waste grounds. Rattle! New Cross Station. Shock! There we were at Croydon. Bur-r-r-r! The tunnel. . . .

After long darkness, pale fitful streaks of light appear. . . . The streaks grow stronger—become continuous—become the ghost of day—become the living day—became I mean—the tunnel is miles and miles away, and here I fly through sunlight, all among the harvest. . . .

Bang! We have let another Station off, and fly away regardless. Everything is flying. The hop-gardens turn gracefully toward me, presenting regular avenues of hops in rapid flight, then whirl away. So do the pools and rushes, haystacks, sheep, clover in full bloom delicious to the sight and smell, corn-sheaves, cherry-orchards, apple-orchards, reapers, gleaners, hedges, gates, fields that taper off into little angular corners, cottages, gardens, now and then a church. Bang, bang! A double-barrelled Station! Now a wood, now a bridge, now a landscape, now a cutting, now a—Bang! a single-barrelled Station— there was a cricket-match somewhere with two white tents, and then four flying cows, then turnips—now the wires of the electric telegraph are all alive, and spin, and blurr their edges, and go up and down, and make the intervals between each other most irregular: contracting and expanding in the strangest manner. Now we slacken. With a screwing, and a grinding, and a smell of water thrown on ashes, now we stop!

Smog hovers over Albert Square in Manchester. The spiky monument to Prince Albert (*left*) was built in the 1860s.

TWO

THE URBAN ENVIRONMENT

The footsteps of a *busy* crowd, the crunching wheels of machinery,
the shriek of steam from boilers, the regular beat
of the looms, the heavy rumble of carts. . . .
Day and night the city echoes with street noises.
~ ALEXIS DE TOCQUEVILLE, *JOURNEYS TO ENGLAND AND IRELAND* (1835)

THE BOOMING INDUSTRIAL CENTERS OF VICTORIAN
England were the first modern cities. They were full of energy and
excitement. They were noisy, dirty, smelly, and downright hazardous
to the health.

The Victorians regarded their cities with a mixture of pride and
horror. Many people were appalled by the wretched working conditions in factories and the sprawling slums where the poor were
housed worse than animals. At the same time, they could not help
being dazzled by the seemingly endless vitality of England's great
urban centers. "Manchester streets may be irregular," wrote one vis-
itor, "its smoke may be dense, and its mud ultra-muddy, but not any
or all of these things can prevent the image of a great city rising
before us as the very symbol of civilization."

A WALK THROUGH MANCHESTER

To get an idea of what a Victorian city looked like, we might step back in time to 1850 and take a walk through Manchester. Our journey begins in the southern outskirts of this thriving industrial town in northwest England. Here we can see a farmer tending his fields. Over there mounds of earth mark the site of a brickworks, where workers dig for the clay used to make bricks for construction projects. Clusters of villas are rising in an area of green trees and pastures. These handsome mansions, complete with large, carefully laid-out gardens, are meant for Manchester's well-to-do bankers, merchants, and professional men. On a nearby street, builders are hammering away at rows of identical connected houses. These cozy "terrace houses" will be home to the business managers and civil servants who will commute into the city by train.

Moving closer to Manchester, we pass through a slightly less prosperous neighborhood. Here the detached houses have small gardens or none at all, and the terrace houses are plainer and more densely packed. This suburban neighborhood is still in sight of the countryside, but it has more of a city feeling. The bustling main streets are lined with shops and pubs. Morning and evening, the streets rumble and clatter with the sound of people traveling to and from work by foot, carriage, or horse-drawn omnibus.

As Victorian cities grew, rows of modest terrace houses sprang up in the suburbs.

Now we are nearing the city proper, and the scene changes once again. First we find ourselves in an area where manufacturing rules. There are cotton mills, sawmills, and an ironworks. These industries are located near busy canals, where we might spot a narrow boat carrying goods to the nearby seaport of Liverpool. The railways are beginning to take over some of the canal trade. Stone-and-iron viaducts pass over the streets, carrying trains to and from the new stations rising throughout the city. Following the path of a viaduct, we walk past a jumble of mills, lumberyards, warehouses, stables, inns, pubs, and crowded back-to-back terrace houses.

At last we reach the historic center of Manchester. Here the narrow unpaved streets give way to cobblestone lanes. There are fine old stone buildings: the stately Cathedral, the large and elegant Town Hall, the massive Exchange where business of all kinds is transacted.

The Irwell River, flowing through the center of Manchester, was an important trading route during the Victorian Age.

There are busy street markets, where merchants in shops and stalls sell fruit, vegetables, meat, poultry, fish, and flowers. Even amid these old-time scenes, we can see signs of the times. Beside the Exchange is an office for the new electric telegraph company. Smoking mill chimneys loom over the Cathedral tower. And sandwiched among all the solid structures devoted to government, business, and industry are pockets of dirty, tumbledown working-class housing.

MANSIONS AND SLUMS

Our tour of Manchester has shown us a city in the midst of a great transition. The Industrial Revolution brought similar changes throughout England. The rapid increases in population and industry led towns to expand in a pattern much like the growth rings on a tree. City centers became a mishmash of old and new public and commercial buildings. Surrounding this district was a thick band of factories, workshops, warehouses, railway yards, and business offices. On the outskirts of the cities, open land and once-isolated towns and villages developed into suburbs.

Industrialization also brought about a growing gulf between the social classes. Before the Industrial Revolution, most towns were so small that people of different classes lived fairly close to one another. As workers poured into the new industrial centers, the classes began to separate. The rich escaped the rising congestion by moving to their country estates or building tall, spacious mansions in exclusive city neighborhoods. Members of the growing middle class moved to the suburbs or to the "better" streets on the cities' outer rings. Depending on their income, they might live in scaled-down versions of the detached houses of the wealthy or in terrace houses. The best terrace houses were three- or four-story structures built in single rows, with small front lawns or a shared parklike garden.

Meanwhile, most working-class people lived in slums sandwiched among the factories and rail yards in the older parts of cities. Some slum housing was created from existing buildings that had been abandoned by better-off people in their flight to the suburbs. Landlords converted these old houses into tenements, renting out the rooms to poor families. In some tenement apartments, as many as twelve members of an extended family lived together, with adults and children crowding into a single bed or sleeping on the floor.

Bedford Park, a fashionable London suburb, had spacious houses with gardens, as well as its own church, shops, pub, and art school.

Other workers lived in "purpose-built slums"—grim districts of housing erected by factory owners or profit-seeking builders, using the cheapest materials and workmanship. Makeshift slum buildings were jammed into every available piece of land, from backyards to alleys to the open space between existing buildings. Many of these dwellings were terrace houses built back to back. Cramped and dreary, the back-to-back houses typically had two tiny rooms, with no ventilation and little or no light.

Cramped and dark, terrace houses in city slum districts were dismal places.

Worst of all the slum dwellings were the cellar rooms. Thousands of poor families in Manchester, Liverpool, Leeds, and other cities were forced to make their home in the damp, dark cellars of slum tenements. One physician who called on a new mother in a cellar dwelling in Liverpool was appalled to find the woman and her newborn child "lying on straw in a vault . . . with a clay floor. . . . There was no light or ventilation in [the cellar] and the air was dreadful. I had to walk on bricks across the floor to reach her bedside, as the floor itself was flooded with stagnant water."

THE SMELLY UNDERBELLY

Sanitation was practically nonexistent in the slum districts of early Victorian cities. Cheap working-class houses had no toilets or running water. As many as forty families might have to share a single privy (outhouse) set in an alley or courtyard. Rather than use these overflowing commodes, many people simply collected their waste in buckets or "slop jars," then dumped it out the window or into cesspools, gutters, or old sewers designed to carry off rainwater. It was not unusual for a city street to become a muddy creek running with human waste, along with droppings from the ever-present horses, the pigs and chickens that many former country people kept in their houses, and the sheep and cattle that were driven through the streets to market.

The noxious mixture from streets and cesspools often made its way into the nearest lake, stream, or river. So did chemical waste from factories. A government commission in Leeds found that the Aire River was "full of refuse from water closets [toilets], cesspools, privies, . . . wastes from slaughter-houses, chemical soap, gas, [and] dye-houses . . . ; there were dead animals, vegetable substances and occasionally a decomposed human body."

Filthy rivers like these served as a source of water for hundreds of thousands of people. Most poor city dwellers got their water from street-corner pumps. A slum district might have one pump for every twenty or thirty tenement houses. Working-class families stood in line to fill their buckets with brown, foul-smelling water, which they used for drinking, cooking, and washing. Upper- and middle-class Victorians were somewhat more fortunate. Their water might come from private storage tanks or wells, or it might be piped into the home by a water company. However, even these sources were often contaminated.

The air of Victorian cities was as unhealthy as the water. Factories, workshops, and coal-burning home fireplaces spewed forth an endless stream of smoke, dirt, odors, and gases. The polluted air caused headaches, sore throats, and nausea. It blackened streets, buildings, furniture, and clothing. To Charles Dickens, London's frequent "fogs" (really smog) looked like "a soft black drizzle, with flakes of soot in it as big as full-grown snowflakes—gone into mourning, one might imagine, for the death of the sun."

A young working-class man sells baked goods on the streets of London.

THREE

THE WORLD of WORK

It was a town of machinery and tall chimneys. . . .
It contained several large streets all very like one another, . . .
inhabited by people equally like one another, who all went in and out
at the same hours, with the same sound upon the pavements,
to do the same work, and to whom every day
was the same as yesterday and to-morrow.
&~CHARLES DICKENS, *HARD TIMES* (1854)

SOCIAL CLASS WOVE ITS WAY INTO EVERY ASPECT OF Victorian life. We have seen how it influenced where and how people lived in England's growing cities. Class also revealed itself in a host of other ways, including clothing, diet, speech, manners, and education.

A person's class was determined partly by birth and partly by occupation. The son of an aristocrat was born at the top of the social ladder. People who worked with their "brains," not their hands, were considered middle class. Those who made their living by manual labor belonged to the working classes. Within each of the classes, there were several different layers. To the Victorians, the distinctions among all these groups were clear and very important. However, they were not fixed in stone. In fact, the Industrial Revolution would bring significant changes to England's traditional class system.

FASHIONABLE FOLK

On a Sunday in 1860, the gentleman barrister (lawyer) Arthur Munby took a stroll through London. As always, the streets of the capital were thronged with men, women, and children of every description. Like most other Victorians, Munby had no trouble categorizing these diverse people by their class and occupation:

> In Fleet St. and the Strand, small tradesmen strolling with wives and children, servant maids with their sweethearts, clerks in gorgeous pairs: westward, "genteel" people, gentry, "swells" & ladies, till the tide of fashionable strollers breaks on Hyde Park Corner: then . . . middleclass men & women staring idly over the blinds of their suburban windows, and slinking back when you look that way: lower class [men and women] standing & staring [out] their doors, equally idle, but much more frank and at their ease; staring openly & boldly, having purchased rest and tobacco by a good week's wages.

The "fashionable strollers" that Arthur Munby encountered in western London belonged to the upper classes. They may have been aristocrats, who held titles and lands that had been in the family for generations, or "gentry," who inherited land but no titles. These people received income from their land and investments, not from paid employment.

The wealthy often divided their time between country estates and grand homes in the best parts of London. While they were in the city, they might go riding in the morning, then spend the rest of the day visiting friends, shopping, and attending dinners, balls, the theater, the opera, and other entertainments. Many upper-class men pursued careers in Parliament. Women might fill their spare hours with "good works." Here is how one aristocratic lady described a "very busy day" in London:

> At 10 1/2 I paid a flying visit to the workhouse. Soon after 11 went . . . shopping for the [Orphans'] Convalescent Home. . . . Luncheon, and at 2 1/2 I drove off to Westbourne Terrace to call on Mrs Martineau. . . ; visited [an aunt] who was out, and Lady Albermarle . . . [went] to Paddington [station] to meet [a relative] but, being a few minutes late, missed her. And finally we dined at Lady Estcourt's.

Aristocratic ladies and gentlemen mingle in London's Hyde Park.

THE STRIVING MIDDLE CLASS

In early nineteenth-century England, the middle class was comprised of a relatively small collection of well-to-do professionals. By the end of the century, it would include a large number of people in a variety of occupations, who altogether made up about 25 percent of the population. Members of this growing class were roughly divided into two main groups, upper and lower. Behind the growth of both groups were the financial opportunities arising from the Industrial Revolution.

The upper middle class included men in older professions such as law, medicine, and banking, who saw their fortunes rise with the increases in population and business. New technologies also opened up prestigious careers in fields such as civil engineering (concerned with the design and building of bridges, dams, and other public projects). Filling out the ranks of the upper middle class were top military officers, university professors, clergymen, and government leaders, as well as the merchants and industrialists who built factories, shipyards, and other large-scale businesses.

The lower middle class encompassed an even broader range of occupations. There were midlevel business managers and civil servants, shopkeepers and shop assistants, foot soldiers, policemen, governesses, and schoolteachers. A great horde of lower-middle-class clerks commuted each day from the suburbs to the city. Nearly anyone who worked in an office was called a clerk, whether his job involved keeping financial records, copying out letters by hand, or preparing complex business documents.

From the junior clerk to the most successful banker, all middle-class people shared a common ambition: to rise up the social ladder. In the new industrial society, an ambitious person could make more money than ever before. Wealth brought a new level of respectability. It meant buying a carriage, perhaps even a country estate. It meant sending your sons to the best schools and marrying your daughters to landed gentlemen. It meant that the best things in life no longer belonged to the high-born only, but to anyone with the talent and drive to achieve them.

The pursuit of wealth and respectability was the driving force behind many of the remarkable advances of the Victorian era. The ambitions of the middle class also shaped the values of their age— values such as discipline, self-reliance, thrift, and, above all, hard work. To the ever-striving Victorians, idleness was a sin and work was practically a divine obligation. The artist and philosopher John Ruskin observed that the "removal of the massy barriers which once separated one class of society from another" had made it almost "shameful" to remain in the middle class. "Now that a man may make money, and rise in the world, . . . it becomes a veritable shame to him to remain in the state he was born in, and everybody thinks it is his *duty* to try to be a 'gentleman.'"

CRAFTSMEN, HOUSEMAIDS, AND FACTORY WORKERS

About three out of every four Victorians did manual work. Like the middle class, the working-class segment of society was divided into layers. The most fortunate were the artisans, or skilled workers, who made up about 15 percent of the working-class population. This elite group included printers, typesetters, carpenters, masons, shoemakers, and other highly trained people in traditional trades, as well as specialists in new fields such as machine and engine repair. Skilled workers enjoyed higher wages and steadier employment than other laboring people. In fact, a printer or builder often made more money than a lower-middle-class clerk—although the clerk could still look down his nose at the man engaged in manual labor.

The majority of working-class people were semiskilled workers. These people learned their skills on the job rather than through formal training. Semiskilled men and women worked in mining, fishing, construction, weaving, dressmaking, and other manual trades. Many were domestic servants in the homes of upper- and middle-class families. Even a small middle-class household would hire a maid-of-all-work to do the cooking and cleaning and look after the children. The very wealthy employed a small army of servants: housekeepers, butlers, cooks, maids, valets, footmen, and others. A servant's hours were long, and the wages were low. One teenage girl who did all the housework and looked after five children for a middle-class couple in London was "often so tired . . . that I fell asleep on the stairs on my way

A laundry maid presses linens with a flatiron, which she has heated on a stove or fire.

Men, women, and children alike worked in Victorian mills and factories.

to bed." Still, for this girl and many like her, domestic service ensured a decent place to live and regular meals.

Hundreds of thousands of semiskilled workers were employed in factories, mills, and workshops. As the nineteenth century progressed, factories produced an ever-wider variety of goods, from cotton and metal products to pickled meats and canned vegetables. Some factory owners took pride in operating clean, safe facilities. In general, though, working conditions were brutal. During the early Victorian period, many factory workers labored twelve or fourteen hours a day, six days a week. The noise could be deafening. The air might be filled with cotton dust, metal fragments, or hazardous chemicals, causing a host of deadly diseases. Long hours spent hunched at the same machine, performing the same task over and over, numbed the hands and deformed the body. In addition, there was the constant danger of crippling accidents when weary workers operated powerful machinery.

Factory hands generally earned just enough to pay the rent and buy food and fuel. There was little left over for clothes and other necessities, nothing at all for saving. When a breadwinner was sick or injured and couldn't work, a couple often had to choose between heat or food, between feeding themselves or their children. Layoffs or an unexpected expense such as medical or funeral bills could plunge an entire family into poverty.

DOWN AND OUT IN THE CITY

The lowest level of the lower class was made up of people with no particular trade or training. These unskilled workers scraped out a living by doing whatever work was available. A young man might become a day laborer, unloading ships at the docks or digging ditches. A woman might take in washing, sewing, and mending. Street vendors sold a wide assortment of goods from their carts and baskets: raw fish, fruit, and vegetables; prepared soup, puddings, and pies; flowers, matches, and watch chains. Dustmen collected the ashes from people's fireplaces. Crossing sweepers swept the filth from city streets so that ladies could cross without getting their skirts dirty. Mudlarks waded in sewage-flooded rivers, seeking lumps of coal, copper nails, and other saleable treasures.

A street vendor sells "fancy-ware"— cheap jewelry, hair combs, and other ornaments.

Thousands of down-and-out people turned to petty crime, prostitution, or begging. Beggars thronged the streets of every city, crying out for coins by day and huddling in doorways or railway tunnels by night. Many were children who had lost their parents. The French historian Hippolyte Taine, arriving in London in 1858, was horrified to find the richest city in the world "alive with 'street-boys,' barefooted, filthy, turning cartwheels for a penny. They swarm on the stairs down to the Thames, more stunted, more livid [bruised], more deformed, more repulsive than the street urchins of Paris."

Most workhouses had separate dining halls for men, women, and children. The residents were seated in rows, all facing the same way, to discourage conversation.

For the beggar or unemployed laborer facing starvation, there was a place of last resort: the workhouse. Workhouses provided needy people with food and lodging in return for labor. In most cases the lodging was no worse than the typical lower-middle-class dwelling. The food was nutritious, if not particularly generous or appetizing. However, the treatment of workhouse inmates was often harsh and humiliating. In the Victorian view of things, the workhouse had to be as uninviting as possible, in order to discourage the "undeserving poor" from relying on public assistance instead of their own efforts. Families who entered the workhouse were split up. Residents had their heads shorn and their clothing exchanged for coarse uniforms. They spent their days toiling at hard, mindless tasks, such as breaking up stones for gravel or "picking oakum"—unraveling tar-saturated ropes into fibers for use in caulking ships.

Worst of all was the shame attached to going into the workhouse. Most working-class men and women would "submit to the greatest privations," observed the English journalist James Grant,

> rather than submit themselves to the degradation of crossing the threshold of a workhouse. From circumstances which have come under my own personal observation, I am convinced that there are hundreds of our mechanics [laborers] and working men who perish every year of absolute want, from their extreme horror of the workhouse.

OLIVER TWIST AND THE WORKHOUSE

The best-known portrait of life in a Victorian workhouse comes to us from the pages of *Oliver Twist*. This famous novel by Charles Dickens tells the story of an orphan boy raised in a dark and dismal London workhouse. In the following passage, Dickens uses an ironic style to describe the attitude of the workhouse's board of guardians toward the unfortunate people forced to rely on their grudging charity.

The members of this board were very sage [wise], deep, philosophical men; and when they came to turn their attention to the workhouse, they found out at once, what ordinary folks would never have discovered—the poor people liked it! It was a regular place of public entertainment for the poorer classes; a tavern where there was nothing to pay; a public breakfast, dinner, tea, and supper all the year round; a brick and mortar elysium [paradise], where it was all play and no work. "Oho!" said the board, looking very knowing; "we are the fellows to set this to rights; we'll stop it all, in no time." So, they established the rule, that all poor people should have the alternative . . . of being starved by a gradual process in the house, or by a quick one out of it. With this view, they contracted with the water-works to lay on an unlimited supply of water; and with a corn-factor [a trader in grains] to supply periodically small quantities of oatmeal; and issued three meals of thin gruel a day, with an onion twice a week, and half a roll [on] Sundays. They . . . kindly undertook to divorce poor married people . . . ; and, instead of compelling a man to support his family, as they had theretofore done, took his family away from him, and made him a bachelor! There is no saying how many applicants for relief . . . might have [come from] all classes of society, if it had not been coupled with the workhouse; but the board were long-headed [farsighted] men, and had provided for this difficulty. The relief was inseparable from the workhouse and the gruel; and that frightened people.

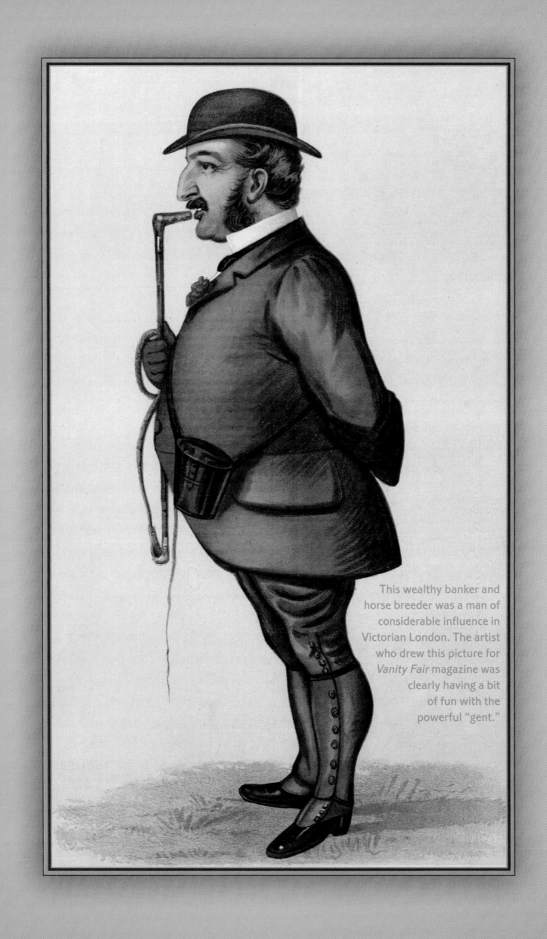

This wealthy banker and horse breeder was a man of considerable influence in Victorian London. The artist who drew this picture for *Vanity Fair* magazine was clearly having a bit of fun with the powerful "gent."

FOUR

THE MEN of THE CITY

If the morning be fine, the pavement of the Strand and Fleet Street looks quite radiant with the spruce clerks walking down to their offices, governmental, financial, and commercial.
∽ GEORGE AUGUSTUS SALA, *TWICE ROUND THE CLOCK* (1859)

ONE OF THE MANY CONTRADICTIONS IN QUEEN Victoria's realm was the fact that a nation with a strong woman on the throne was, in nearly all other instances, dominated by men. Only men could vote in parliamentary elections or hold office in the national government. Men also enjoyed the greatest educational and employment opportunities. As a result, the middle-class profession-als and clerks who flooded city streets each morning were, until late in the Victorian period, all male.

At home the man was the "king of the castle"—whether that "castle" was a splendid city mansion, a snug suburban terrace house, or a cramped tenement apartment. For the pious Victorians, a mar-ried couple's proper relationship was summed up nicely in a biblical passage: "For the husband is the head of the wife. . . . [W]ives should submit in everything to their husbands."

TOP HATS AND WORKMEN'S CAPS

In 1797 a men's clothing dealer named John Hetherington caused a commotion by wearing a top hat on the streets of London. According to some accounts, the new style was such a shocking sight that several passersby booed and four women fainted. Hetherington was arrested on a charge of disturbing the peace by "wearing upon his head a tall structure having a shining lustre and calculated to frighten timid people."

Two decades later, top hats were so common that no respectable middle-class urban male would have ventured outdoors without one. Made of stiff canvas covered mainly with felt or silk, "toppers" were hot, uncomfortable, and impractical. Rain and rough handling ruined them. A stiff breeze could topple them. When a hat was past its prime, the owner might sell it to a used clothing dealer, who spruced it up and resold it. Photographs from early Victorian times show a wide range of men wearing top hats, from well-to-do gentlemen to middle-class clerks to laborers digging up roadways. Later in the century, the rounded bowler hat also became popular with men of all classes.

The hat was just one element of a wardrobe designed to make the Victorian male appear serious and gentlemanly. Upper- and middle-class men typically wore white linen shirts with high, stiff collars. The shirt was topped by a dark-colored waistcoat buttoned up nearly to the chin. Over these layers went either a black "frock coat"—a wool coat that came down to the knees—or, on formal occasions, a dress coat with long tails. Wool trousers, usually gray or black, were held up by suspenders. Leather gloves and a silk neck cloth called a cravat, tied in a knot or bow, might add a splash of color to this somber outfit. Every respectable man also carried a cane, walking stick, or tightly furled umbrella, a carryover from the days when gentlemen wore swords as a sign of their high birth.

Working men's clothes were usually made of cotton, which was less costly than wool or linen. Laborers often wore short jackets instead of frock coats, and many topped their heads with cloth caps. So many workmen bought their clothes secondhand that one study of London life noted, "In England all classes, except the agricultural, dress alike with a difference. Observe [the] lemonade vendor. His dress is that of a prosperous middle-class man—gone to shreds and patches."

By the end of the Victorian period, factory-made clothes were becoming more widely available. Better-off people, who were used to having their clothes custom made, sneered at ready-made clothing. For many working men, though, these less expensive garments made it possible to dress more comfortably, warmly, and fashionably.

Working-class men might wear top hats or bowlers, just like more well-to-do gentlemen.

This mock magazine cover, based on an issue of the *Illustrated Police News*, was created for a British television series about Jack the Ripper. The series was produced in 1988, exactly one hundred years after the still-unsolved murders.

JACK THE RIPPER

The policeman's top hat of black varnished leather was a familiar sight on the streets of early Victorian London. The Metropolitan Police Force had been founded in 1829 by the head of Britain's Home Office, Sir Robert Peel. The members of the force, nicknamed "bobbies" or "peelers," were armed with truncheons (short clubs) and a wooden rattle (later replaced by a whistle). The bobbies patrolled the city streets, checking shop doors and shining their lanterns into dark alleys. They proved so effective at deterring crime that Parliament decided to establish similar police forces throughout the country.

The police could not prevent all crime, of course. Pickpockets still swarmed in city streets, filching handkerchiefs, purses, and pocket watches. Other criminals snatched silk hats from people's heads, plucked laundry from clotheslines, burglarized homes and shops, and committed more violent crimes. Beginning in August 1888, London reeled under its most shocking crime spree: the brutal murder and mutilation of several prostitutes in slum districts. A series of taunting letters (including one enclosed with part of a human liver) were sent to the police and newspapers. The letters were signed "Jack the Ripper." While historians believe that most, if not all, of the letters were hoaxes, their publication made the murders a national sensation.

The public's reaction to Jack the Ripper revealed widespread racial and class prejudices simmering just below the surface of Victorian life. Many upper- and middle-class people were convinced that the murderer belonged to the "weak and passionate" lower classes. Another common theory was that Jack was a foreigner—most likely one of the Jewish immigrants from Russia or Germany who made up a small but growing minority in eastern London. The *Manchester Guardian* reported that "all are united in the belief that [the killer] is a Jew or of Jewish parentage." The *London Times* endorsed the idea that only an outsider could have committed the murders, because "the celerity [speed] with which the crimes were committed is inconsistent with the ordinary English phlegmatic [restrained] nature."

The Metropolitan Police questioned hundreds of suspects, but they never caught Jack the Ripper. In November 1888 the murders stopped as suddenly as they had started. Although the case has been officially closed for more than a century, modern-day historians are still debating the identity of England's most notorious serial killer.

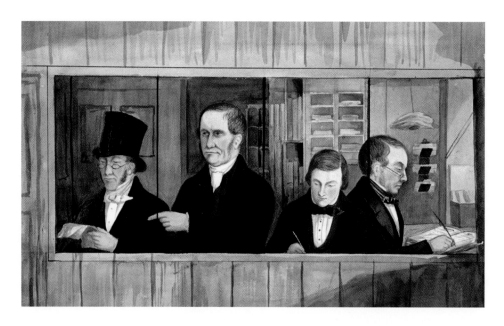

A DAY IN THE LIFE OF A CLERK

A manager examines the work of the clerks in a Victorian business office.

It's Monday morning, and hordes of workers are making their way into London. If you were a young man employed as a clerk, you would grab a quick breakfast and join the "rush hour" traffic. All around you, a silent army of men trudges in from the suburbs, crossing the fields, detouring around the houses and brickworks. The middle-aged men are an unbroken sea of dark gray and black. Some of the younger ones cut a more dashing figure, with gloves and cravats in pea green, rose pink, and other startling colors.

Once you reach the city proper, the crowds begin to separate. Some men stroll down the pavement, while others climb into omnibuses or horse-drawn cabs on their way to more distant legal, government, or business offices. Your destination is a countinghouse on London's Fleet Street, where you help keep track of business for a successful printing company.

Your work is not difficult, but it can be dull. You share the small countinghouse with two other clerks, and as the youngest among them, you usually get the most tedious tasks. All morning you perch

on a high stool, bent over a sloping desk. By the dim light of an oil lamp, you copy out letters, invoices, and other business documents with a goose-quill pen, dipped from time to time in an inkwell. The noise of the presses and workmen makes a busy hum outside the countinghouse door, growing to a noisy clatter each time a messenger goes in and out on an errand.

Top-hatted clerks commute by omnibus in nineteenth-century London.

By noon, your stomach is growling. The company owner takes his lunch at a coffee shop or chophouse, while the laborers buy sausages, potatoes, and other "fast food" from street vendors. You and your fellow clerks usually make do with something from home. Today you've brought a cheese sandwich, which you eat as you work. During the afternoon, you'll snack on the pack of sweet biscuits (cookies) tucked away in your desk drawer.

The clock chimes six. Your workday is done. Slapping on your top hat, you hurry back out to the dingy, smog-shrouded streets. This is the hour when many professional men go to gentlemen's clubs, exclusive enclaves with handsome dining rooms and libraries. Working-class men have their own clubs and pubs, where they can enjoy

A middle-class family enjoys a quiet evening at home (perhaps not quite as tranquil for their cat and goldfish).

a beer at the end of a long day. Meanwhile, *you* head straight home to your family. You enjoy a quiet dinner, then an hour of reading out loud to your wife and young children. Like other middle-class Victorians, you regard home as a peaceful refuge from the hustle and bustle of the business world.

Such is your life six days a week, Monday through Saturday. Sunday is a day of rest, spent attending church and relaxing with your family. (Later in the Victorian period, "short Saturdays" will give you an extra half day off.) In your free time, you may do some volunteer work, sitting on your local church council or a committee for a charitable organization. You also look forward to your annual unpaid holiday, usually a family trip to the seashore.

As your career progresses, you will strive to move up the ranks from junior to senior clerk. You will make sure your sons get a good education and your daughters find respectable husbands. If your employer is generous, you may end your working days with a bit of savings, perhaps even a small pension. No matter how well you do, though, you will never quite shake the fear of losing everything you have worked so hard to attain.

For that is the flip side of the Victorian male's dominance. Along with his privileges come weighty responsibilities. He must be manly and strong, the tireless breadwinner and protector of his family. Above all, he must avoid what the novelist Mary Ann Evans (better known by her pen name, George Eliot) described as "the disgrace and misery of 'failing,' of losing all one's money, and being ruined,— sinking into the condition of poor working-people."

An elegantly
dressed Victorian
woman enjoys her
afternoon tea.

FIVE

"THE ANGEL in the HOUSE"

Man for the field and woman for the hearth:
Man for the sword, and for the needle she:
Man with the head, and woman with the heart:
Man to command, and woman to obey;
All else confusion.

∾ ALFRED, LORD TENNYSON, *THE PRINCESS* (1847)

BOOKS AND MOVIES SOMETIMES GIVE THE IMPRESSION that Victorian women were delicate creatures who spent their days sipping tea and doing embroidery. This image mixes up the middle-class ideal of womanhood with the actual facts of everyday life. As we have seen, the Victorians lived in a male-dominated society. In their view, men and women were designed to occupy "separate spheres," with men more suited to the harsh public world of business and politics and women destined for the private sphere of home. The ideal wife, in the words of a popular poem, was "the angel in the house." Selfless and virtuous, she devoted her life to making a happy home for her family. She ran the household but never forgot that her husband was its true master. Drawing on her inborn "feminine" qualities, she instilled religion and morality in her children and inspired her husband to ever-greater virtue.

For many Victorian women, this ideal was unrealistic. Millions of lower- and middle-class women had no choice but to take paying jobs, both in and outside the home. Even for full-time homemakers, running a large household took lots of "unladylike" hard work.

The puffy bustle, trailing skirt, and striped polonaise (a bodice and over-skirt in one garment) date this lady's clothes to the late Victorian period.

CORSETS AND CRINOLINES

A Victorian woman's clothing reflected her position in society. Women of the upper and upper-middle classes advertised their family's wealth by wearing dresses made from costly fabrics, in the most up-to-date fashions. Tight-fitting sleeves and shoulders made it clear that the wearer could not possibly lift her arms to do physical work. Fancy ruffles, bows, and fasteners showed that she had servants to help her dress and take care of her wardrobe.

A typical Victorian day dress included a long skirt and a matching long-sleeved bodice. A tightly laced corset beneath the dress gave the wearer a fashionably tiny waist (along with the inability to take a deep breath or move about comfortably). During the early Victorian period, skirts gradually became wider as women took to wearing five or six layers of stiff petticoats. In the 1850s the petticoats were replaced by the crinoline, a bell-shaped frame of whalebone or steel that fluffed out the skirt, while making it hard for women to sit down or pass through a doorway. This ridiculous fashion accessory soon gave way to the bustle, a padded cushion at the back of the skirt that supported a cascading train of fabric.

Depending on the occasion and the family's income, dresses might be made of wool, linen, velvet, or silk. Fabrics came in a great variety of colors: white, pale gray, dark greens and browns, vivid blues and purples. Women always wore a bonnet or hat when they went outdoors. They coiled their hair in a bun or piled it artfully on top of the head. Respectable women wore little or no makeup. One magazine writer urged girls in the market for a husband to think twice before using "those slight aids to beauty. . . . I have known several courtships brought to untimely halts by eye-black running [and] rouge rubbing off on to pale waistcoats."

Wealthy ladies had their clothing specially made by a dressmaker. A middle-class woman on a tight budget might buy the fabric for a dress, pay the dressmaker to cut and fit it, then stitch the pieces together herself. Working-class women made their own clothes or bought them secondhand. As the Victorian era progressed, the sewing machine and the availability of ready-made clothes put fashion within the reach of all but the poorest women.

WOMEN AT WORK

In 1841 a former textile worker named William Dodd described the life of an eighteen-year-old Manchester "factory girl": "She takes a drink of cold coffee, . . . a mouthful of bread (if she can eat it), and having packed up her breakfast in her handkerchief, hastens to the factory. The bell rings as she leaves the threshold of her home. Five minutes more, and she is in the factory. . . . The clock strikes half-past five [5:30 a.m.]; the engine starts, and her day's work commences."

Two hours later, Dodd continued, the machine slowed down, and the young woman cleaned it and "swallowed a little food." She worked on until noon, when she hurried home for a quick lunch. "This done, it was time to be on her way to work again, where she remains, without one minute's relaxation, till seven o'clock; she then comes home, and throws herself into a chair exhausted. This repeated six days in the week. . . . This young woman looks very pale and delicate, and has every appearance of an approaching decline."

Young women like William Dodd's factory worker were certainly aware of the Victorian ideal of womanhood, but it had little relevance to their day-to-day lives. Women made up roughly one-third of the regular paid labor force in Victorian England. The great majority of female laborers came from the working classes. Most were employed in traditionally female fields, such as domestic service, textile and clothing production, and laundry cleaning. Working-class women also held a wide variety of other jobs: bookbinder, brewer, brick maker, butcher, potter, trash collector, used clothing dealer.

A secondhand clothing shop in a poor section of Victorian London

Working-class women's wages were a vital part of the household income, going toward necessities such as food and rent. In contrast, middle-class wives and daughters often worked so that the family could afford fine clothes, elegant furnishings, and other luxuries that maintained the appearance of respectability. A middle-class woman might earn extra income by doing piecework in her home, making handmade goods such as lace, hosiery, or gloves. She might help out in the family business, handling clients, correspondence, and bookkeeping. A single woman could work as a governess, tutoring the children in a wealthy household. In the final years of the Victorian period, an increasing number of middle-class women worked as shop assistants, clerks, civil servants, teachers, and nurses.

No matter where women worked, conditions were hard. Factory

women put in the same long hours as men, in the same unhealthy, uncomfortable surroundings. Shop assistants might have to stand behind a counter seventy-five or more hours a week. (Most shop owners did not provide seats for workers until Parliament passed a law in 1912 requiring them to do so.) In all fields, from factory work to teaching, women were paid less than men doing the same jobs. In addition to their paying jobs, most working women also shouldered all or most of the household responsibilities. The pioneering nurse Florence Nightingale described the result of this double burden: "Women never have half an hour in all their lives (excepting before and after anybody is up in the house) that they can call their own."

WOMEN AT HOME

The ideal middle-class home was clean, comfortable, and elegant. The servants were well managed. The children were well cared for. The household accounts were always in order, and the family never lived beyond its means. The "angel in the house" achieved all this while remaining calm and cheerful and *never* troubling her husband with domestic concerns.

Even a woman with one or more servants could have a hard time living up to these ideals. Most middle-class city houses were tall and narrow, with several floors to trudge up and down. Fireplaces and oil lamps coated the rooms with soot that had to be cleaned off every day. There was a *lot* to clean, because the Victorians loved to stuff their homes with decorative furniture, plush carpets, fussy curtains, and an endless array of knickknacks. There were no vacuum cleaners or mechanical washing machines and few of the other laborsaving devices that make household chores easier today.

The mistress of a middle-class household usually met with the servants each morning to organize the day's household tasks. She planned the menu and ordered food from the tradespeople who called at the kitchen door. In the days before refrigeration, many perishable goods had to be bought fresh daily.

The homemaker might spend the rest of the morning taking care of the household correspondence and paying the bills. She was also responsible for designing the rooms, buying the furnishings, and hiring and supervising workmen for renovations and repairs. She made sure everyone in the family always had the right clothes, in the best possible condition. She served as her children's first tutor, teaching them the alphabet and, just as importantly, the manners and values that would help them take their proper place in society.

In addition to all these duties, the model homemaker had to keep up with the family's social obligations. That included arranging dinner parties, calling on other ladies, and receiving her own callers. Middle-class women also helped organize and raise funds for a wide variety of charitable causes. There were benevolent societies to deal with nearly every social ill, from alcoholism to slum housing to destitute widows and orphans.

In the mid-nineteenth century, some female charity workers turned their attention to their own concerns, giving rise to the women's rights movement. These early feminists demanded better wages and working conditions for working-class women, better educational and employment opportunities for middle-class women, and greater legal and political rights for women of all classes. Their efforts would gradually lead to improvements in women's status, along with changes in the Victorian ideal of womanhood. "The good old days, when our grandmothers worked samplers and studied their recipe books, have passed away," wrote one observer in 1888. "The present generation of girlhood, with enlarged ideas as to woman's brain and woman's work, is standing on the threshold of life eager to mingle in life's warfare."

ENGLISH TEA SCONES

The Victorians ate three main meals a day: breakfast, luncheon, and dinner. They also enjoyed a late-afternoon meal that they called "tea." At teatime a few ladies (and sometimes gentlemen) gathered in a friend's drawing room. The maid brought in a tray laden with a china teapot, cups and saucers, sugar, cream, and lemon slices. Next came an assortment of bite-size sandwiches, sweets, and pastries.

The recipe below makes a dozen scones—a rich, biscuitlike pastry often served at afternoon tea. For an authentic Victorian tea, set the table with dainty china plates, small napkins, spoons, and butter knives. Arrange the warm scones on a serving platter, along with plenty of butter and jam. And, of course, don't forget to offer your guests a cup of freshly brewed black tea!

2 cups all-purpose flour

2 tablespoons sugar

2 1/4 teaspoons baking powder

1/2 teaspoon salt

6 tablespoons unsalted butter, cut into pieces

1 small egg

1/2 cup whole or 2-percent milk

1. Preheat the oven to 400°F.

2. Place the flour in a medium-size mixing bowl. Stir in the sugar, baking powder, and salt.

3. Rub the butter into the flour with your fingers until the mixture resembles coarse crumbs.

4. Beat the egg lightly in a separate small bowl. Stir in the milk.

5. Make a well in the center of the flour. Pour in the milk, and stir with a fork just until the mixture begins to stick together.

6. Turn the dough out onto a lightly floured cutting board. Dust your hands with flour, and knead the dough about ten times, until it is nearly smooth.

7. Pat the dough into a flat circle and roll lightly with a floured rolling pin, to make a circle about three-quarters of an inch thick.

8. Cut the dough into twelve rounds with a two-inch cookie cutter. (Gather and reroll the scraps as needed.) Place the rounds about one inch apart on a baking sheet dusted with flour. Bake for 15 to 20 minutes, or until golden brown. Be sure to use pot holders or an oven mitt when handling the hot baking sheet.

This upper-class girl's toy collection would have made her the envy of many less fortunate Victorian children.

SIX

A VICTORIAN CHILDHOOD

Children should be seen, not heard.

∽A POPULAR SAYING IN VICTORIAN TIMES

THE PEOPLE OF VICTORIAN ENGLAND HAD LARGE families. The average family included six children, and about one-fifth of all families had ten or more. Life was perilous for all these boys and girls. There were no vaccines for common childhood diseases such as measles and whooping cough. The young were also vulnerable to the epidemics of cholera, typhoid, and other diseases that periodically swept through England's dirty, crowded cities. Even late in the century, when improvements in sanitation and health care had begun to reduce the country's overall death rate, about 155 of every 1,000 babies died before their first birthday.

The death rates were highest among working-class families, who often could not afford proper health care and nutrition for children

The faces of the children in this family photo reflect the hardships of life in a London slum.

and pregnant mothers. In the slum districts of cities such as Manchester, half of all children died before the age of five. For those who survived, social class and income would continue to play a major role in many areas of life.

LIFE IN THE NURSERY

Privileged boys and girls grew up in the nurseries of wealthy Victorian homes. The nursery was a room in a separate part of the house where the children were cared for by a professional nanny (or, in less prosperous middle-class households, a nursery maid). It was the nanny or nursery maid who fed and dressed the children, who cared for them when they were sick and comforted them when they were unhappy. Refined Victorian parents loved their offspring—but at a distance. They believed, as one nineteenth-century novelist explained, that it was the nanny's job to "have the *trouble* of the children, their noise, their romping; in short, let the nursery be her place, and the children's."

On a typical day in a well-to-do urban home, the nanny roused her young charges around eight o'clock and brought them down to the dining room, where the father led the entire household in morning prayers. Then the children went back up to the nursery for breakfast, while their parents ate downstairs. After breakfast the nanny took the youngsters to the park, where they could play with boys and girls of their own class. The rest of the morning was spent in lessons, followed by lunch, nap time, more playtime, and afternoon tea.

Around five o'clock young children ate their supper in the nursery. Then the whole family gathered for the "children's hour." In some households this was a time for games and storytelling. Stricter parents expected their sons and daughters to dress up and practice making polite conversation. At the end of the hour, the youngsters were trundled upstairs to bed. In upper-class households this meant that children might see their parents for little more than an hour all day. In less affluent middle-class homes, the mother played a somewhat more active role in her children's lives, overseeing their lessons

The man of the house leads his wife, daughter, and servants in morning devotions.

and minding them for a few hours each day while the nursery maid took care of other chores.

The structured routine of a Victorian childhood was designed to accomplish two goals. It freed the parents for their own pleasures and obligations, while providing a sheltered environment in which children could learn the virtues of order, self-discipline, and obedience. Parents and nannies were quick to punish any signs of rebellion, sometimes with a whipping, more often with a stern lecture. It was only sensible, wrote the English novelist Samuel Butler, to stifle "the first signs of self-will" while children were "too young to offer serious resistance. If their wills were 'well broken' in childhood, . . . they would acquire habits of obedience which they would not venture to break through."

PETTICOATS AND BREECHES

As part of their strictly regimented upbringing, upper- and middle-class children ate a bland diet consisting mainly of bread, porridge, and well-boiled meat and vegetables. Rich foods and sweets were thought to be bad for a child's delicate stomach. Even worse, eating food just because it tasted good might encourage a willful self-indulgence.

A little boy in a skirted sailor suit, photographed around 1880

Children's clothing could be as unpleasant as their diet. Both boys and girls wore dresses until around age five. After that, girls wore scaled-down copies of their mother's clothes, complete with many layers of underwear and petticoats. Their brothers might be dressed in miniature sailor suits, Scottish kilts, or short jackets paired with long trousers. Late in the Victorian era, many boys had to endure the "Little Lord Fauntleroy" costume. This was a black velvet suit with lace at the collar and cuffs that was inspired by the young hero of a popular novel published in 1886. One six-year-old boy managed to get out of wearing this "infernal get-up" by "flinging myself down in the gutter . . . and cutting the breeches."

Despite the fussy clothes and strict rules, a childhood spent in the nursery was not all disagreeable. There were always plenty of toys: dolls and dollhouses, rocking horses, toy soldiers, model trains and ships, jigsaw puzzles, board games. There were a wealth of books, including some of the first novels written specially for children, such as Lewis Carroll's *Alice's Adventures in Wonderland*, Anna Sewell's *Black Beauty*, and Louisa May Alcott's *Little Women*. For outdoor play there were kites, hoops, rubber balls, jump ropes, and seesaws. Many children also had a pet dog or cat to play with.

The middle-class views of childhood gradually changed as the century wore on. The idea that the convenience of adults should always come first gradually gave way to a more child-centered world. By the end of the Victorian era, it was not uncommon to find parents depriving themselves in order to give their children a comfortable home and the best possible education.

GETTING AN EDUCATION

There was no national school system in early Victorian times. Whether or not a child got an education depended largely on his or her social class, family income, and gender.

For the children of upper- and middle-class families, education began in the nursery. The most prosperous families employed a governess or tutor. In less well-to-do households, mothers gave children their first lessons in reading, writing, religion, and morality.

At around age seven, boys went on to private day schools. These were businesses owned by a single proprietor; for example, an educated widow or retired tutor who taught English, French, history, and other subjects in his or her home. At age twelve or thirteen, many boys were sent to public schools. The public schools (so-called because they had once been open to all) were exclusive boarding schools that charged fees to students. They were run by a corporation or board of governors, who hired the headmaster and teachers. Aristocrats paid large sums to send their sons to prestigious public schools such as Eton and Harrow, where the students spent most of their time studying Latin and Greek. As prosperous members of the rising middle class began to seek out a "gentleman's education" for their sons, some public schools added math, grammar, and other more practical subjects.

The majority of boys left public school after four or five years, although some stayed on to graduate at around age nineteen. After school most young men moved directly on to careers. Some dedicated students continued their education at universities, medical schools, engineering schools, or military colleges.

While well-to-do boys went to school, their sisters usually completed their education at home. Most girls were taught sewing, drawing, and piano playing by their mothers (or, in prosperous households, a governess or tutor). Some attended private day schools or boarding schools for girls. Until late in the century, the curriculum at most girls' schools consisted mainly of fancy needlework, art, music, dancing, and other "feminine" accomplishments.

Children from less prosperous families were often denied even these limited educational opportunities. Skilled workers and struggling clerks might send their children to inexpensive private schools, but such establishments were generally overcrowded, with teachers

A YOUNG CROSSING SWEEPER

The life of a working-class boy or girl was worlds away from the sheltered upbringing in an upper-class nursery. Children were often hungry when they grew up in families with little money and many mouths to feed. They dressed in ragged hand-me-down clothes. As soon as they were old enough, they were put to work. At the start of the Victorian era, children as young as five were employed in mines, factories, and work-shops. Over time Parliament passed a series of laws that set a minimum working age (age twelve by 1901), limited children's hours, and barred them from some industries completely. Even with these reforms, many boys and girls continued to spend many hours laboring over piecework in their homes. Others took care of younger brothers and sisters, worked as servants, or earned a few pennies at odd jobs. The journalist Henry Mayhew interviewed dozens of young laborers in Lon-don, including an enterprising twelve-year-old girl who helped sup-port her family by singing in the streets and sweeping crossings.

I'm twelve years old, please sir, and my name is Margaret R___, and I sweep a crossing in New Oxford Street. . . . Mother's been dead these two year, sir, and father's a working cutler [a maker of cutting tools], sir, and I lives with him, but he don't get much to do, and so I'm obligated to help him, doing what I can, sir. Since mother's been dead, I've had to mind my little brother and sister, so that I haven't been to school; but when I goes a crossing-sweeping I takes them along with me, and they sits on the steps close by, sir. . . . Sister's three and a-half year old, and brother's five year, so he's just beginning to help me, sir. I hope he'll get some-thing better than a crossing when he grows up. . . .

First of all I used to go singing songs in the street, sir. It was when father had no work, so he stopped [stayed] at home and looked after the children. . . .

I used to see men and women, and girls and boys, sweeping, and the people giving them money, so I thought I'd do the same thing. That's how it come about. Just now the weather is so dry, I don't go to my crossing, but goes out singing. . . . I only go sweeping in wet weather, because then's the best time. . . .

I carn't tell whether I shall always stop at sweeping, but I've no [good] clothes, and so I carn't get a situation [a job as a servant]; for, though I'm small and young, yet I could do housework, such as cleaning.

Above: One of the many ragged, hungry working children of the Victorian cities

Working-class children attend a "dame school"—a type of small private school usually run by an older woman in her home.

who might be barely literate themselves. Many other children attended free or low-cost elementary schools operated by religious and charitable societies. The "Ragged Schools" provided poor city children with free meals and clothing, along with instruction in reading, writing, religion, and practical skills such as sewing. Impoverished families often could not spare a working child's wages, however, and most poor boys and girls were lucky to get two or three years of schooling.

EXPANDING OPPORTUNITIES

Throughout the Victorian era, reformers called for an overhaul of England's haphazard and unequal educational system. In 1870 Parliament responded with the Elementary Education Act. This law required that every child have access to an elementary education. Where there were not enough charitable schools to meet children's needs, the government provided funding for buildings and teachers' salaries. Later in the century, additional laws made schooling mandatory up to the age of twelve.

The government-sponsored "national" or "board schools" were administered by locally elected school boards. The educational environment at these institutions was far from ideal. A class might have as many as seventy or eighty children, and the instruction focused mainly on memorization of names, dates, and figures. Well-to-do families continued to send their children to private and public schools instead. Toward the end of the century, these included an increasing number of schools for middle-class girls interested in a more serious education. At these new day schools, boarding schools, and "collegiate" (college-like) schools, girls could study a wide range of subjects such as English literature, history, math, and science.

Meanwhile, many disadvantaged boys and girls were learning to read and write in the board schools. For the most ambitious and hardworking students, the new system offered a chance to break through the barriers of class, income, and gender. The benefits of a free public education would become apparent as increasing numbers of young working-class men and women began to climb the ladder to careers as clerks, engineers, nurses, and teachers.

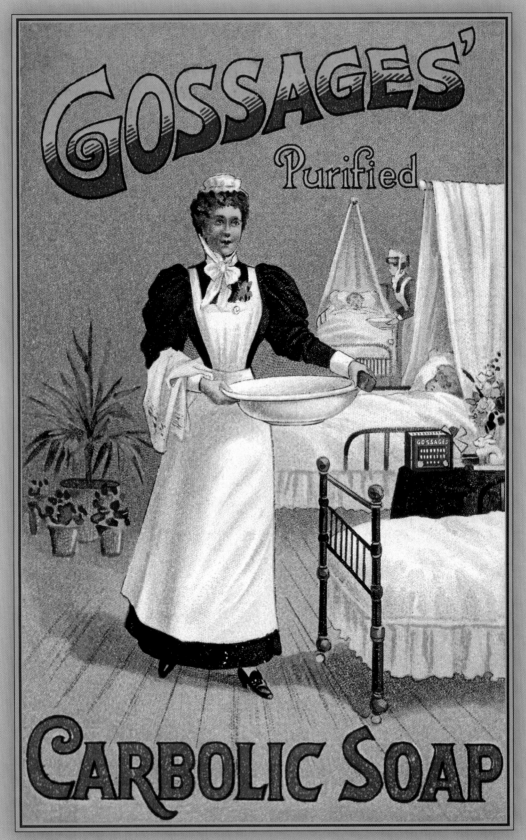

A new emphasis on sanitation reduced death rates in Victorian England's homes and hospitals.

SEVEN

AN AGE OF REFORMS

The Cholera is the best of all sanitary reformers;
it overlooks no mistake and pardons no oversight.

~ LONDON TIMES (1848)

WHEN WE LOOK BACK ON LIFE IN THE VICTORIAN CITIES, it is easy to shake our heads over the widespread filth, poverty, and social inequality. It is worth remembering, though, that the people of nineteenth-century England were confronted with challenges that no one had ever faced before. The explosive growth of their cities had overwhelmed the systems of government and social services passed on by earlier generations. In order to improve the lives of city dwellers, the Victorians would have to rethink their ideas about private rights and reshape their governments. They would have to investigate conditions, pass legislation, and make sure the laws were enforced. In the process they would come up with the first solutions to complex problems that city planners still wrestle with today.

THE PUBLIC HEALTH MOVEMENT

In the 1830s to 1860s, Great Britain was ravaged by four separate outbreaks of cholera. The disease killed more than 125,000 people, with the majority of fatalities in city slums. Just as frightening as the number of deaths was the rate at which cholera killed. About half of those who contracted the disease died of it. A strong young man or woman could feel fine in the morning and be dead by afternoon. More often, victims died after several days of violent stomach cramps, vomiting, and diarrhea.

While cholera inspired the greatest terror, it was far from the only deadly disease to strike England during the Victorian period. Recurring outbreaks of typhoid brought fever and death to one in four victims. Typhus, a separate disease with similar symptoms, killed 16,000 people a year in the late 1830s. There were also recurring epidemics of influenza, diphtheria, and scarlet fever.

Today we know that all these diseases are caused by germs. The people of the filthy Victorian cities contracted cholera and typhoid by swallowing contaminated food and water. Typhus was spread mainly by the body lice that thrived in unsanitary conditions. Overcrowding encouraged the spread of contagious diseases, and malnutrition lowered resistance among the poor.

In early Victorian times, however, most doctors blamed illness on miasma, or "bad air." Recommended treatments included everything from warm baths and bloodletting to worthless concoctions such as "Daffey's Elixir" and "Morrison the Hygienist's Genuine Vegetable Universal Mixture." More useful were attempts to ward off illness by getting rid of the bad air. People who flushed their smelly drains and scrubbed out their houses sometimes managed to get rid of the germs as well.

Clearly, the worst miasma hovered over the poorest sections of London and other cities. In 1839 a government official named Edwin

Chadwick launched a series of investigations into the connection between disease and poverty. Chadwick concluded that the high death rates among the working classes were a result of "atmospheric impurities produced by decomposing animal and vegetable substances, by damp and filth, and close and overcrowded dwelling." Improving sanitation in the cities would save countless lives, he argued. It would also save the government money in the long run, by reducing the unemployment and poverty that frequently followed ill health.

The efforts of Edwin Chadwick and other pioneering reformers marked the beginning of the public health movement. In 1848 Parliament passed the first of several acts establishing national and local agencies to safeguard public health and the environment. Under the new laws, many cities began to clean up their cesspools and drains. Sewage pipes were installed to carry waste to treatment plants. Reservoirs, dams, and aqueducts were built, and pipes were laid to carry clean water to some houses. City streets were paved, and trash collection was organized. Slaughterhouses and livestock markets were moved away from populated areas. City health inspectors worked to ensure that dairies, bakeries, schools, workshops, and other public and private sites met cleanliness standards.

Livestock and poultry markets helped spread disease in crowded urban areas.

By the 1890s, the miasma theory had died out as researchers discovered the organisms responsible for cholera, typhoid, diphtheria, and other diseases. While there were no cures yet, public health measures had dramatically reduced the rate of infection and death.

It had taken a terrifying series of epidemics and a terrible loss of life, but the public had gradually come to accept the role of government in improving society. That acceptance was part of a new spirit of reform that was also transforming many other aspects of city life.

FROM UGLY TO (ALMOST) BEAUTIFUL

Housing reform was an essential part of the public health movement. The Victorians had recognized that the filth and overcrowding in city slums bred disease. Just as important to many reformers was the belief that slum conditions contributed to immorality. "It is to no purpose to preach from the pulpit," asserted Lord Shaftesbury, a member of Parliament and leading reformer, "so long as you leave the people in this squalid, obscene, filthy, disgusting, and overcrowded state."

At first some cities dealt with their worst slums by demolishing them. This only made the problem worse, as displaced people were forced to move into the remaining slum housing, now even more crowded. Efforts by a few prosperous business owners and social reformers were more helpful. The successful industrialist Sir Titus Salt moved his textile mill from the growing city of Bradford to a pleasant site in the countryside, where he built an entire village for his workers. The village, called Saltaire, had a hospital, school, park, and more than eight hundred roomy houses, each with clean piped-in water and an outside commode. Angela Burdett-Coutts, one of the richest women in England, built a neighborhood of model tenements in eastern London. The housing project transformed an area of dung heaps and tumbledown cottages into four blocks of clean, airy apartment buildings set around grassy squares.

There were also numerous government attempts to improve housing for the poor. Beginning in the early 1840s, several cities passed building codes and other legislation regulating housing. Manchester,

Leeds, and Birmingham banned new construction of the cramped, airless back-to-back terrace houses. Liverpool led the way in combating the appalling conditions in cellar dwellings, closing some of them and ordering landlords to make others fit for human habitation. At the national level, Parliament passed laws empowering local authorities to inspect dwellings, demolish dangerous buildings, and purchase land for the construction of decent working-class housing.

Titus Salt built the model community of Saltaire on the banks of the Aire River in northern England.

All these efforts met with strong resistance from landlords and others who opposed government interference with private property. Well into the twentieth century, there were still slum dwellings in nearly every major English city. Nevertheless, conditions were improving. In 1900 a character in a novel by George Sims returned to London after a long absence and was surprised to see change "in every direction."

> Narrow streets have yielded to broad, handsome thoroughfares; whole areas that were once little better than slums have been cleared, and vast hotels and splendid shops stand where, only a few years back, the thieves and ruffians of London herded. . . . From being one of the ugliest cities in Europe, London has, during the last fifteen years, been transformed into one of the most beautiful.

PROGRESS AND CHALLENGES

An English city dweller standing on the brink of the twentieth century could look back with some satisfaction. Along with their public health and housing reforms, the Victorians had tackled a multitude of other urban problems. They had taken the first steps toward reducing air pollution from factories, mainly through fines imposed on offenders. Working conditions in factories were slowly improving, due to new regulations aimed at safeguarding workers' health and limiting their hours. Trade unions had been legalized, giving the workers a powerful tool in their struggle for better wages and working conditions.

Other government reforms had extended voting rights to nearly all urban working men. Women would not gain the right to vote in parliamentary elections until 1918. However, the final years of the Victorian era did bring laws allowing them to control their own property and earnings, to serve on school boards and other local government agencies, and to vote in local elections. Meanwhile, thanks to the new board schools, collegiate schools for girls, and other institutions, education was no longer a privilege reserved for men of the upper classes.

The Victorian era also saw considerable progress in the fields of science and medicine. The English surgeon Joseph Lister introduced the "antiseptic method," which enabled doctors to perform operations under sterile conditions, reducing the risk of infections. Florence Nightingale revolutionized the nursing profession, improving nurses' training and hospital conditions. Newly discovered anesthetics made surgery and childbirth less painful. Increasing numbers of hospitals, infirmaries, and public health services were being established in London and other cities.

Due to all these developments and more, the men and women who came of age during the last quarter of the Victorian period were

VICTORIAN AGE FIRSTS

The Victorian period was a time of remarkable advances in science and technology. Here are just a few of the many inventions and discoveries made in England, France, Italy, the United States, and other countries, which transformed life in ways great and small.

Antiseptic surgery

Aspirin

Can opener

Chloroform

(used as an anesthetic in surgery)

Chocolate bar

Contact lenses

Dynamite

Electric light bulb

Ironclad warship

Motion pictures

Motor car

Pasteurization

Phonograph

Photography

Postage stamp

Radio

Refrigerator

"Safety bicycle"

(first bicycle with two wheels the same size)

Sewing machine

Subway

Suspension bridge

Telegraph

Telephone

Typewriter

X-ray

Zipper

Above: The invention of the typewriter in 1867
opened up many office jobs for women.

better off than their parents had been. They were earning higher wages. Advances in transportation and factory production were making food, clothing, and other consumer goods more affordable. Workers had more leisure time, with the new half day on Saturday and four national holidays established by Parliament. In their free hours, they could relax in the public parks, athletic fields, museums, libraries, and concert halls springing up in many prosperous cities.

This more comfortable life did not apply equally to all people. At the end of the nineteenth century, cities were still searching for solutions to a host of thorny problems: continuing air pollution, a shortage of clean water, pockets of overcrowded slum dwellings, a large population of working-class people who remained just one step ahead of poverty. But the energetic, self-confident, optimistic Victorians had no doubt that they were equal to the challenge. "There is much in what we see around us that we may easily and rightly wish to see improved," observed the *London Times* in January 1901, as the death of Queen Victoria brought the Victorian Age to a close.

> But no permissible deductions can obscure the fact that the period in question has been one of intellectual upheaval, of enormous social and economic progress, and, upon the whole, of moral and spiritual improvement. . . . If we now enter upon our work in a spirit embodied in the untiring vigilance and the perpetual openness of mind that distinguished the queen, . . . her descendants will witness advances not less important than that of her long and glorious reign.

GLOSSARY

barrister A lawyer who is permitted to present cases in England's higher courts.

bodice (BAH-diss) The upper part of a woman's dress.

cholera (KAH-luh-ruh) An acute disease that attacks the intestines and is usually contracted by consuming contaminated food or water.

civil servants People who work in government departments.

corset A women's undergarment fitted with strips of whalebone or another stiff material. The corset was laced up to give the appearance of a small waist.

countinghouse An office in which a business carries on operations such as accounting.

gleaners Workers who gather up the remaining bits of grain and other crops after the harvest.

hops A plant grown mainly for its flowers, which are used in making beer.

Industrial Revolution The historical period marking the introduction of power-driven machinery and the social changes that resulted. The Industrial Revolution began in England in the mid- to late 1700s.

miasma A quality or vapor in the air, once believed to cause illness.

omnibus A public vehicle designed to carry passengers. In early Victorian times, omnibuses were pulled by teams of horses.

Parliament The national legislature of Great Britain.

tenements Run-down apartment buildings. Victorian landlords often converted old houses into tenements, dividing the rooms into apartments and renting them out to lodgers.

terrace houses Identical houses built in a row, which are connected so that each house shares its side walls with a neighbor or neighbors.

typhoid An acute disease that attacks the intestines. Typhoid fever is contracted by consuming contaminated food or water or by coming into close contact with an infected person.

viaduct A long elevated roadway supported on arches, piers, or columns.

FOR FURTHER READING

Ashby, Ruth. *Victorian England.* New York: Marshall Cavendish, 2003.

Brocklehurst, Ruth. *Victorians.* London: Usborne Publishing, 2004.

Chrisp, Peter. *A History of Fashion and Costumes: The Victorian Age.* New York: Facts on File, 2005.

Damon, Duane C. *Life in Victorian England.* New York: Thomson Gale, 2006.

Ferguson, Sheila. *Growing Up in Victorian Britain.* London: B. T. Batsford, 1984.

Mitchell, Sally. *Daily Life in Victorian England.* Westport, CT: Greenwood Press, 1996.

Price-Groff, Claire. *Queen Victoria and Nineteenth-Century England.* New York: Marshall Cavendish, 2003.

Swisher, Clarice. *Victorian England.* San Diego, CA: Lucent Books, 2001.

———. *Women of Victorian England.* San Diego, CA: Lucent Books, 2005.

Yancey, Diane. *Life in Charles Dickens's England.* San Diego, CA: Lucent Books, 1999.

ONLINE INFORMATION

All Change in the Victorian Age. Bruce Robinson, British Broadcasting Corporation.
www.bbc.co.uk/history/british/victorians/speed_01.shtml

Children in Victorian Britain. British Broadcasting Corporation.
www.bbc.co.uk/schools/victorians/

Ford Madox Brown's "Work." (Interactive exhibit exploring an important Victorian Age painting of working-class life.) Manchester Art Gallery.
www.manchestergalleries.org/ford-madox-brown

Lend Me Your Ears: Victorian London. BBC Radio 4, British Broadcasting Corporation.
www.bbc.co.uk/radio4/history/lend_me_your_ears.shtml

London History: Victorian London. Britain Express.
www.britainexpress.com/London/victorian-london.htm

Time Traveller's Guide to Victorian Britain. Channel 4, London.
www.channel4.com/history/microsites/H/history/guide19/index.html

Who Were the Victorians? Woodlands Junior School, Tonbridge, Kent, England.
www.woodlands-junior.kent.sch.uk/Homework/victorians.html

SELECTED BIBLIOGRAPHY

Arnstein, Walter L. *Britain Yesterday and Today: 1830 to the Present.* 8th ed. Boston: Houghton Mifflin, 2001.

Avery, Gillian. *Victorian People in Life and in Literature.* New York: Holt, Rinehart, and Winston, 1970.

Begg, Paul. *Jack the Ripper: The Uncensored Facts.* London: Robson Books, 1990.

Briggs, Asa. *Victorian Cities.* New York: Harper and Row, 1965.

Broomfield, Andrea. *Food and Cooking in Victorian England: A History.* Westport, CT: Praeger, 2007.

Davies, Jennifer. *The Victorian Kitchen.* London: BBC Books, 1991.

Dickens, Charles. *Selected Journalism: 1850-1870.* Edited by David Pascoe. New York: Penguin Books, 1997.

Dyos, H. J., and Michael Wolff, eds. *The Victorian City: Images and Realities.* Vol. 1. London: Routledge and Kegan Paul, 1973.

Flanders, Judith. *Inside the Victorian Home: A Portrait of Domestic Life in Victorian England.* New York: W. W. Norton, 2004.

Holcombe, Lee. *Victorian Ladies at Work.* Hamden, CT: Archon Books, 1973.

Houghton, Walter E. *The Victorian Frame of Mind, 1830-1870.* New Haven, CT: Yale University Press, 1957.

Paterson, Michael. *Voices from Dickens' London.* Cincinnati, OH: David and Charles, 2006.

Picard, Liza. *Victorian London: The Life of a City, 1840-1870.* New York: St. Martin's, 2005.

Pike, E. Royston. *"Golden Times": Human Documents of the Victorian Age.* New York: Frederick A. Praeger, 1967.

Pool, Daniel. *What Jane Austen Ate and Charles Dickens Knew.* New York: Simon and Schuster, 1993.

Wohl, Anthony S. *Endangered Lives: Public Health in Victorian Britain.* Cambridge, MA: Harvard University Press, 1983.

SOURCES FOR QUOTATIONS

ABOUT VICTORIAN ENGLAND

p. 6 "Since it has pleased": Queen Victoria, *Queen Victoria in Her Letters and Journals*, edited by Christopher Hibbert (New York: Viking, 1985), p. 23.

p. 7 "an age of transition": Sir Henry Holland, "The Progress and Spirit of Physical Science," *Edinburgh Review*, July 1858; quoted at www.archive.org/stream/essaysonscientif00hollrich/essaysonscientif00hollrich_djvu.txt

CHAPTER 1: THE WORKSHOP OF THE WORLD

p. 9 "Our country": Robert Vaughan, *The Age of Great Cities* (London: Jackson and Walford, 1843), p. 92.

p. 13 "*Then* was the old": William Makepeace Thackeray, "De Juventute," 1860; quoted in Houghton, *Victorian Frame of Mind*, p. 3.

p. 15 "radically altered": *London Times*, October 5, 1869; quoted in Briggs, *Victorian Cities*, p. 20.

p. 17 "Ah! The fresh air": Dickens, *Selected Journalism*, p. 139.

CHAPTER 2: THE URBAN ENVIRONMENT

p. 19 "The footsteps": Alexis de Tocqueville, *Journeys to England and Ireland*, 1835; quoted in Alexis de Tocqueville, *Alexis de Tocqueville on Democracy, Revolution, and Society*, edited by John Stone and Stephen Mennell (Chicago: University of Chicago Press, 1982), p. 306.

p. 19 "Manchester streets": *Chamber's Edinburgh Journal*, vol. 9, 1858; quoted in Briggs, *Victorian Cities*, p. 83.

p. 20 Description of Manchester around 1850 adapted largely from G. F. Chadwick, "The Face of the Industrial City: Two Looks at Manchester," 1973, in Dyos and Wolff, *Victorian City*, pp. 247-256.

p. 24 "lying on straw": "Royal Commission on the State of Large Towns and Populous Districts," 1845; quoted in Wohl, *Endangered Lives*, p. 297.

p. 25 "full of refuse": J. Toft, *Public Health in Leeds in the Nineteenth Century* (master's thesis, University of Manchester, 1966); quoted in Wohl, *Endangered Lives*, p. 235.

p. 25 "a soft black drizzle": Charles Dickens, *Bleak House*, at http://ebooks.adelaide.edu.au/d/dickens/charles/d54bh/chapter1.html

CHAPTER 3: THE WORLD OF WORK

p. 27 "It was a town": Charles Dickens, *Hard Times*, 1854, at http://ebooks.adelaide.edu.au/d/dickens/charles/d54ht/chapter5.html

p. 28 "In Fleet St.": Derek Hudson, ed., *Munby: Man of Two Worlds, The Life and Diaries of Arthur J. Munby 1828-1910* (London: John Murray, 1972); quoted in Flanders, *Inside the Victorian Home*, p. 29.

p. 29 "very busy day": John Bailey, ed., *The Diary of Lady Frederick Cavendish* (London, 1927); quoted in Picard, *Victorian London*, p. 110.

p. 30 "removal of the massy": John Ruskin, "Pre-Raphaelitism," 1851; quoted in Houghton, *Victorian Frame of Mind*, p. 187.

p. 31 "often so tired": M. L. Davies, ed., *Life As We Have Known It* (London, 1931); quoted in Picard, *Victorian London*, p. 121.

p. 33 "alive with 'street-boys,'": Hippolyte Taine, 1858; quoted in Avery, *Victorian People*, p. 218.

p. 34 "submit to the greatest": James Grant, *Sketches in London*, 1838, at www.victorianlondon.org/publications/sketchesinlondon-7.htm

p. 35 "The members of this board": Charles Dickens, *Oliver Twist*, 1838, at http://ebooks.adelaide.edu.au/d/dickens/charles/d54ot/chapter2.html

CHAPTER 4: THE MEN OF THE CITY

p. 37 "If the morning": George Augustus Sala, *Twice Round the Clock; or, the Hours of the Day and Night in London* (London: Houlston and Wright, 1859); quoted in Flanders, *Inside the Victorian Home*, p. 30.

p. 38 "For the husband": Ephesians 5:23-5:24.

p. 38 "wearing upon his head": quoted at http://news.bbc.co.uk/1/hi/england/london/4527223.stm

p. 39 "In England all classes": Gustave Doré and Blanchard Jerrold, *London: A Pilgrimage* (London: Anthem Press, 2005; first published 1872), p. 38.

p. 41 "weak and passionate": *Eastern Argus*, September 8, 1888; quoted in Begg, *Jack the Ripper*, p. 72.

p. 41 "all are united": *Manchester Guardian*, September 10, 1888; quoted in Begg, *Jack the Ripper*, p. 79.

p. 41 "the celerity": *London Times*, October 4, 1888; quoted at http://etext.virginia.edu/journals/EH/EH35/haggard1.html

p. 42 The description of a day in the life of a clerk is adapted largely from Paterson, *Voices from Dickens' London*, pp. 81-99.

p. 45 "the disgrace and misery": George Eliot, *The Mill on the Floss*, 1860, at www.online-literature.com/george_eliot/mill_floss/22/

CHAPTER 5: "THE ANGEL IN THE HOUSE"

p. 47 "Man for the field": Alfred, Lord Tennyson, *The Princess* (1847), part 5, lines 437-441, at http://theotherpages.org/poems/tenny12.html

p. 47 "The Angel in the House": poem by Coventry Patmore, 1854, at www.gutenberg.org/etext/4099

p. 49 "those slight aids": quoted in Picard, *Victorian London*, p. 103.

p. 49 "factory girl" and "She takes a drink": William Dodd, *The Factory System Illustrated* (London: John Murray, 1842), at www.umassd.edu/ir/resources/workingconditions/w30.doc

p. 51 "Women never have": Florence Nightingale, "Cassandra," 1852, in Florence Nightingale, *Cassandra and Other Selections from Suggestions for Thought*, edited by Mary Poovey (New York: New York University Press, 1993), p. 213.

p. 52 "The good old days": Charles Dickens Jr., "Artistic Professions for Women," *All the Year Round*, Sept. 29, 1888; quoted in Holcombe, *Victorian Ladies at Work*, p. 194.

p. 53 The kitchen-tested recipe for English Tea Scones is loosely adapted from Davies, *Victorian Kitchen*, p. 180.

CHAPTER 6: A VICTORIAN CHILDHOOD

p. 55 "Children should be seen": This common saying appears in many sources, including Edward, Duke of Windsor, *A King's Story: The Memoirs of the Duke of Windsor* (New York: G. P. Putnam's Sons, 1951), p. 28.

p. 56 "have the *trouble*": Mrs. Henry Wood, *East Lynne* (Whitefish, MT: Kessenger Publishing, 2004; first published 1861), p. 383.

p. 58 "the first signs": Samuel Butler, *The Way of All Flesh* (New York: Penguin

Classics, 1986; first published 1903), p. 53.

p. 59 "infernal get-up": Compton Mackenzie, *My Life and Times*, Octave One, 1883-1891 (London: Chatto and Windus, 1963); quoted in Sarah Levitt, *Victorians Unbuttoned* (London: George Allen and Unwin, 1986), pp. 102-103.

p. 61 "I'm twelve years old": Henry Mayhew, *London Labour and the London Poor*, vol. 2 (New York: Dover Publications, 1968; first published 1861-1862), pp. 505-506.

CHAPTER 7: AN AGE OF REFORMS

p. 65 "The Cholera": *London Times*, September 5, 1848; quoted in Wohl, *Endangered Lives*, p. 117.

p. 66 "Daffey's Elixir": Wohl, *Endangered Lives*, p. 121.

p. 67 "atmospheric impurities": Edwin Chadwick, *Report on the Sanitary Condition of the Labouring Population of Great Britain*, 1842; quoted in Wohl, *Endangered Lives*, p. 147.

p. 68 "It is to no purpose": Lord Shaftesbury, *The Labourers' Friend*, July 1853; quoted in Wohl, *Endangered Lives*, p. 7.

p. 69 "in every direction": George R. Sims, *In London's Heart* (New York: Buckles and Company, 1900), pp. 49-50.

p. 72 "There is much": *London Times*, January 23, 1901; article reproduced in G. M. Young, *Victorian England: Portrait of an Age* (New York: Oxford University Press, 1964), p. 156.

INDEX

ABOUT THE AUTHOR

VIRGINIA SCHOMP wrote her first short story (starring a magical toad) in kindergarten. She spent the rest of her school years with her nose in a book, pulling it out just long enough to earn a Bachelor of Arts degree in English Literature at Penn State University. Following graduation, she worked at several different publishing companies, learning about the day-to-day details of writing and producing books. After fifteen years of helping other writers realize their dreams, she decided that it was time to become a published writer herself. Since then she has written more than seventy books for young readers on topics including dinosaurs, dolphins, occupations, American history, ancient cultures, and ancient myths. Ms. Schomp lives in the Catskill Mountain region of New York, where she enjoys hiking, gardening, watching old movies on TV and new anime online, and, of course, reading, reading, and reading.